Words of Life's
Journey

Sheila Goudeau

BookLeaf
Publishing

Words of Life's Journey © 2023

Sheila Goudeau

Presentation by *BookLeaf Publishing*

Web: www.bookleafpub.com

E-mail: info@bookleafpub.com

ISBN: 9789358368970

First edition 2023

DEDICATION

This book is dedicated to all those who think and dream beyond themselves!

ACKNOWLEDGEMENT

I would like to thank God for His gift to me of being able to express myself through writing. I would like to thank my children for being my inspiration. And special thanks to my daughter, Christina, for her priceless help and work in making this book possible.

PREFACE

Writing poetry came naturally to me at an early age. I was 8 years old when I wrote my first poem. Very quickly, I had written several more - simple poems that a child would write, but interesting and fun to use words that rhymed to convey a thought, picture, or experience. I like to see the world and my life experiences in an artistic way. Poetry is that medium of expression for me! Off and on, over the last 60-plus years, I have written poems. And now I have completed a book of poetry. You can see, through my eyes, so many things that are common to us all. Being a mother, grandmother, great-grandmother, world traveler, and teacher has given me a wide and deep perspective on life, and I am grateful to share them with you.

Odd For a Girl

I dreamed of exploring the Amazon,
Or digging up pyramids sounded like fun!
I was only 8 years old,
But had big dreams; bold!
Not the usual dream of a little girl,
Just interested to explore the world.
At first, I aspired to be a nun;
I wanted to serve God and Jesus His Son.
Always a little outside of the box,
What most consider normal, I am not.
I definitely walked to a different beat,
Sometimes it backfired and caused defeats.
I'm in a kind of transition right now,
I will spend the years I have left;
Perhaps they will end up being the best!

Old Friends

It's wonderful to talk to old friends,
After 50 years, view life from a different lens.
We were young, didn't know very much,
But life experience seasoned us as such.
And now we talk, wisdom and understanding,
Came from a lifetime of discovery unending.
Of simple truths found in friends and flowers,
Sunrises, sunsets, winds and powers;
That God manifests on any given day,
For now, that's all I have to say!

Joys of Reading

I really love to read!
Each book plants a seed.
New thoughts to ponder,
Sometimes I just let my mind wander.
Imagine taking a liking,
To the history of a Viking.
Or travel to exotic places,
And seeing different faces.
A good book is like watching a movie,
As we said in the 60's - "really groovy."

Election 2020

Of all the craziness 2020 has wrought,
An election year that has been fraught.
With the worst division, hostility ever seen,
Fueled by fear, mistrust, a derailed train it
seems.
Who is telling the truth? Who cares about our
lives?
Is it integrity or just popularity for which they
strive?
This country is a wild horse, loose from its stall,
Can anyone really fix it - make it better for all?
Some will say maybe it's too late,
Neither candidate can change the fate;
Of a country that's largely chosen money over
God,
And now all this trouble! Shouldn't seem so odd!
The Oval Office will be occupied by one man,
Who "wins" this election in this troubled land.
I think we all better start to pray,
For hope, peace in our streets, a better day!
No man can really fix what's wrong,
We will need God's favor if we are to continue
on!

Should Have Kept It Shut

Seems we opened Pandora's box,
Would have been better kept under locks.
How an ill wind blows worldwide,
Demons and men; puffed up with pride.
Don't they see their end is near?
The writing on the wall is very clear!
Time is running out to get it right,
But it's not too late! Not the "night".
Open your hearts to what is true,
You will find a "new you."
There is peace, also love,
Humility opens heaven above;
And sends answers here on Earth,
To save us all from this dearth.

It Rained Today

I always liked rainy days,
Sleeping late, a chance to laze.
It was the relaxing sound,
Of thunder and the rain falling down;
Set the tone for indoors,
Reading, board games, coloring; we sat on the floors.
Hot tomato soup, sandwiches, grilled cheese,
Made the day special, if you please.
I also like the days of sunshine,
But rainy days never made me whine.
I still love hearing the rain,
Even walking in it, can't complain.
After all, nothing green would ever grow,
Without the rain to nourish it so.
We have food to eat, beauty to behold,
In wondrous forests, truth be told.
We need the rain, it's a life-giver,
For crops, every pond, lake and river.

How Do You Think I Feel?

I felt like crying because they hate me,
I tried so hard to show the love.
But still yet they couldn't get free,
Nor grow in faith in Him up above.

And in prayer, I heard, "How do you think I feel?"
On the evil and the good I send rain,
Yet they hate me too and refuse to kneel;
Fighting, bitter, supposing revenge is gain.

My spirit still tries to soften their hearts,
Hoping they notice blessings here and there;
And realize they are still a part,
Of My divine purpose, and that I care.

So, I prayed, "Please open their eyes!"
To the Truth of Your certain Presence;
No need to wait til one dies,
To know You, and all that is gracious.

Island Girl

Something magical; beckoning wave,
Thoughts of her land, and when she had to be
brave.
To leave the "Aloha" to start a new life,
Thousands of miles away; dealing with the
strife.
Of a new land, new experience, new faces,
But she can never completely erase the traces.
Her island roots remain strong,
Walking towards the waves, she hears the song;
Of waterfalls, rainbows, exotic flowers,
She becomes aware of her inner power.
That gives her the strength to recreate,
Aloha where she is, with her son and her mate.

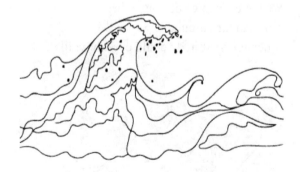

What in the World?

The condition of the world today
Is disheartening and cold; what can I say?
Hatred and division are the popular stance,
Harsh speech and anger have increased violence.
People no longer really want peace,
Nor resolution or arguing to cease.
Seems the majority relish a fight,
Creating arguments for nothing and thinking
they're right.
I don't want to be a part of this kind of mess,
Want to head to the mountains; find a way to
bless.
Want to be healthy and whole,
Mind, body, spirit, and soul.
Can my light shine for others to see?
We have a choice of how to be.
This can turn around if we will,
A change in attitude could cure these ills.

Current Events

Sitting on a wall,
Thinking about it all.
"What's goin' on", I said,
Too many people ending up dead.
Is there help? Is there hope?
Is there a way we can cope?
I look within; Jesus is there,
I ask Him, "Do you care?"
He showed me the scars in His hands,
The tears; He weeps for the lands.
Reminded me He paid a price,
So we don't have to "roll the dice."
It's not a gamble to trust in Him,
Read His word; don't just skim!
Put it in your heart so you will know,
Confidence, peace, stability also.

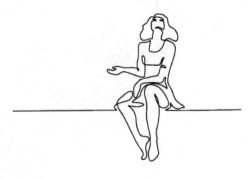

The One

He came like a knight in shining armor,
After so much struggling that took it out of her.
Only wanted to find true love,
The man of her dreams, she looked above.
Asked God to end her sorry plight,
And then he showed up one night.
At a party, she was single; so was he,
And whispers started; Maybe? Can it be?
A love for life, unexpected timing,
But perfect for each other; two souls
intertwining.
Now living out the dream they chose,
Life and love, blooming like a rose.

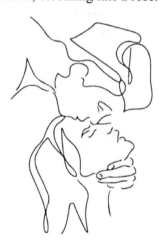

Seasons and Changes

Someone once said, "Life has a middle name",
"Change" is what it is, he claimed.
I have come to believe this is true,
Because life has seasons, brings changes to me
and you.
How boring if every year was the same,
No opportunity for growth, only shifting of
blame.
On others for stagnation in our circumstance,
Or frustration for things out of balance.
"Because they have no changes...they fear not
God",
The Good Book soup, so it's really not odd;
That changes come with each new season,
To celebrate the never-ending trajectory,
Of seasons and changes that make our life story.

Why Do They Act Like That?

It's a different world now,
What is wrong or what they allow.
It's a weakness to be polite,
They say it's better to growl and bite.
Call someone a nasty name,
After all, life is only a game.
It's a selfie culture where the ultimate is me,
True teamwork missing, no mention of we.
Love your neighbor as you love yourself,
Means others are important, not to be put on a shelf.
Using words that lift up, not knock down,
A word is a seed planted, not just a sound.
In conclusion, when put on a scale,
It should be 50/50, others and self won't fail.

Cat in the Woods

Her furry coat is black and white,
She never gets too close, she won't bite.
For many months we have seen sightings,
Of her in the woods, even at dusk in dim
lighting.
We don't know how she eats without living in a
house,
Perhaps catches birds or a field mouse.
Fortunately, there are no poisonous snakes,
Only wooded areas not near any lakes.
Sometimes days pass, we don't see her at all,
She doesn't have a name for us to call.
Even in freezing weather, when we thought she
would die,
We saw her again when sunshine was in the sky.
Hope she lives a really long time,
Because it will justify my silly rhyme.

For Them

After all these years,
After all the effort and tears;
I thought things would be better,
Seems like it all didn't matter.
Anger still in their heart,
They take no responsibility for their part.
Their demands have become extreme,
And pronouncements of judgment are so mean.
I believe they have a clouded mind,
Because of hate in their heart, they always find.
They really don't want God to be Love,
But to punish, no patience with Him above.
I only hope one day light breaks into their soul,
Reveals the unconditional Father's love that
covers all.

I Would Like to Have Known You

We won't meet on this side of life,
The loss cut my heart and soul like a knife.
I can't explain the chasm of empty,
I longed to hold my very own baby.
I take comfort in the certainty,
You are in heaven, growing up in eternity.
I trust we will meet at a later date,
When I am finished here; I won't be late.
At last; embrace; holding you in my arms,
Where no evil can touch us or bring us harm.

For Sandra

It's only knee surgery, no need to fear,
Not your heart, brain, or back; God is near.
The result will be a new knee, no pain,
Enjoy a walk again; sunshine and rain.
I recently had my knee replaced too,
I was nervous but needed to do
The surgery and recovery; You are in my
prayers,
You'll be OK! I know because I've been there!

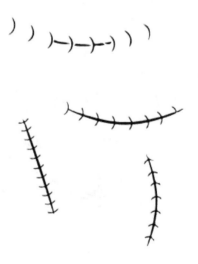

Nature Lover

I love being outside,
In a natural setting beside;
A tall tree or a beautiful flower,
In sunshine or a Spring shower.
Watching different kinds of fowl,
Sporrows, bluejays, peacocks and owls.
Fruit trees, fall with their bounty,
all so wonderful, so much beauty!

I Won't Be Afraid

Fear is a funny thing,
Tells you that uncertainty is king.
Doubt and fear go hand in hand,
The events of this time, in this land;
Are causing the hearts of those far and near,
To be shaken and sick with fear.
I have decided, I won't have that in mind,
Living afraid would put me in a bind.
The impact of all these changes,
My emotions in all the ranges.
Have to come back to the promises I know,
To the unchanging Truth I go.
Trust in God; He controls from above,
It may not look good, but His Love
Will conquer whatever evil may send,
And will reign forever, the world without end.

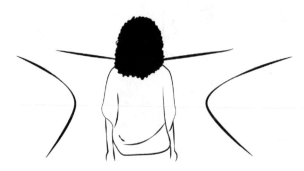

Spring in Lacey

Evergreens against the blue skies,
Sunshine and colors greet my eyes.
Scots broom and pretty foxglove,
Chirping robins heard above.
There is the house finch out in the tree,
Making a nest right in front of me.
Squirrels and rabbits run about,
Days like these make me want to shout.
I can see high up the red-tail hawk,
Searching, soaring, while I walk.
Thoroughly enjoyed this glorious day,
Wish all year could be like this month of May.

Life Time

Life and time are interwoven,
Each of us has days chosen.
Also numbered for a season,
When time is up, we try to find the reason.
Some have life extending for decades,
Others only have days, still they make;
An impact that we remember,
The blessing, although short, left an ember.
"A time to be born, a time to die",
No need to wonder why.
God is in control of life and death,
From our first inhale, to our very last breath.
There is life beyond this life and time,
Some have gone there, seen the divine.
Heaven is a place, it is real,
Doesn't matter how you feel.
One day we will know, as we are known,
When we reach our eternal home.

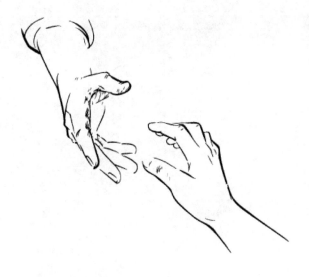

9 789358 368970